DHARMA DRAMA

Dharma Drama

MICHELLE ESBERG

Michelle Esberg

First Printing, 2021

DEDICATION

In honour of my incredible teacher, Sonia Moriceau,
for guiding me to the other shore.

With endless appreciation to Dawn,
who's boundless generosity and friendship
kept me afloat throughout my journey.

And with love to my beautiful wife,
for finding the path that would lead me home.

CONTENTS

MIND THE GAP

Like Velcro, I must cling to you!
Not like a shadow,
Following, or slightly ahead.
That will not do.
I must become one with you,
Merge with you.
Not the smallest gap must separate us,
For it is within these gaps
That fear makes its home,
Drives the wedge between us
And engulfs us completely.

SUFFERING

No matter how fast I run,
I cannot outrun you.
Your patience is infinite,
For no matter how long I sleep,
You are always there to greet me.
You are the master of disguise,
And my many ploys to outwit you are foiled every time.
My efforts to destroy you
Only succeed to tighten your grip upon my heart.
But I am not Jesus,
And you no longer have to be the cross upon my back.
Instead, I shall fashion from you
A shawl of the finest silk,
And wear you draped loosely about my shoulders.
I shall hold you in my hands as I would an injured bird,
And embrace you each moment
As I would a long dead friend.

WHY?

I

If you were to take it from me,
I would not rest for longing.
So why then,
When you give me
What I always dreamed of,
Do I cast it aside like a broken toy?

II

You said this would wake me up,
Rekindle in me the wonder of life.
Why then, does my fascination with death
Return with a vengeance?

NO REASON

She never could find a reason,
And still she can't.
Only now, she has no reason
For seeing no reason,
And no longer a dream to cling to.

WALKING AWAY

She is walking out of her life.
She does not look back.
Like a butterfly emerging from a chrysalis
That has become too tight,
She sheds this dead constraint.
Eyes blinking at the brightness of the light,
She is walking out of her life.
More delicate,
But beneath that vulnerability,
A subtle strength.
She is walking out of her life
But she knows not where she is going.

NOWHERE

There is no place to hide,
No place of refuge exists.
You cannot run fast enough
You cannot climb high enough
And standing still offers no relief.

BEING

There is no way, no path,
No solution, no cure, no way out.
Only a state of being.
Where you position yourself
Within this state of being
Is quite arbitrary.

UNGRASPABLE

I can feel it,
I can touch it
But I cannot grasp it.
It slips through my fingers,
Unsubstantial.

THE LIMPET

You cling to me like a limpet upon my back.
My efforts to prize you off
Leave me exhausted.
Enough! I can fight no more.
I will throw down the towel
And roll out the red carpet.
I will raise my arms in surrender
And embrace you.

THE OCEAN

It's all just a drop in the ocean.
We, and all that we do
Are no more than drops in the ocean.
I will never me any more than the smallest drop.
I will never be any less than the ocean itself.

THE DHARMA

I

What used to be my solace, my refuge,
Has become a millstone round my neck.
I mistook the raft for the river,
The finger for the moon.
And now I am caught in the reeds,
Clinging to the raft that disintegrates around me.

II

You push me, you pull me,
You will not let me rest.
Yet your very seduction
Was to entice me with freedom.

A GENTLE MAN

There was a man, who walked often down this road.
Was he alone as he walked?
Or, as I suspected,
Did he carry his loved ones always in his heart?
Doc Martens he wore,
But it was not they that touched the earth,
But a deep and sincere gentleness
That caressed the ground.
Where did he go to, day in, day out,
This man that walked by my window?
Was he going anywhere?
Had he already arrived?
An amusing thought would often enter my mind.
I saw the worms deep in the earth below.
They would take off their armour
And remove their ear-defenders as this man walked by,
Gentle smiles softening their faces
As ripples of peace and love echoed thorough the soil
And came to rest in their hearts.

MEMENTOS

Boots fashioned from the finest concrete,
I received upon my birth day.
The straightest of jackets I wore,
And a chain was placed about my ankle,
The rusty metal discolouring my skin.
For years I would look up to the sky,
Watching the birds soar,
Watching the clouds float gently by,
And wondering, wishing,
Hoping for the day
When I could shed these mementos of a past life
And finally fly.

CONUNDRUM

You cannot pin the tail upon this donkey,
For she moves too slowly for you to catch her.
No moss will gather upon this stone
As it lies quietly beneath the roots of a tree.
But watch!
See the dust as it settles upon this spinning top.

A FINE LINE

Only the pace has changed,
But alas, the underlying tension remains.
The same gun is at my head,
The knife at my wrist,
And the noose around my neck,
As I try to negotiate the mines underfoot.
It is too fine this line,
Too fine.

LIFE

I

Once you are on, there's no getting off.
Once its begun, it's already too late,
Too late to lament and bemoan.
It is here, it is now.
Through it all
Just find a way to be happy

II

In the morning a day seems too long.
In the evening, a lifetime seems too short.
Can I wake up before I die?

LOST AGAIN

Lost again
No landmarks to define this place.
Just keep on walking

THERE IS A WAY

There is a way,
She said,
But I cannot find it

WILL I EVER KNOW?

I am jealous of your steadfastness,
Your unshakeable belief.
I envy your contentment,
Your undying commitment.
How does it feel to have no doubts?
To be utterly at peace with what you do?
To know that this is enough?
To know in the depth of your heart
That this is it?
Will I ever know?

SHADOWS

Come out of the shadows,
Step into the light,
So I might get a better look at you.
Come now- I mean you no harm.
I just want to see clearly
What has been causing so much pain for so long.

LET ME PICK YOU UP

Let me pick you up,
Feel the fullness of your presence
In every cell of my body.
Let me know with every step,
Every breath that I take,
That you are here with me.
Let me pick you up,
So that I will truly know
When I come to put you down for the last time.

UNTITLED

You wear my clothes,
Respond to my name,
And steal my voice at times.
But how can I complain?
For there are times
When I borrow your eyes to view the world.

BUDDHA

How have I come to be here -
With you perched upon my mantelpiece,
Living my life in your shadow?

HERE WITH ME

You are here with me,
I know you well.
Let us walk together until you depart.
I will not rejoice at your arrival,
Nor lament at your leaving.

SADNESS

I carry you always within me
Your weight lies heavy upon my heart
Slowly crushing me

WINGS

I cannot smash you up,
Nor can I outrun you.
You do not diminish when I expand,
Nor do you crush as I contract.
My screams do not send you running
And my gestures of friendship
Have not managed to unite us.
So, sitting here – what more can I do?
I will give you wings,
And watch you slowly merge
Into the vastness of the sky.
I cannot free myself from you
But I can open my heart
And release you from my grip.

IN SEARCH OF RESONANCE

I can never stand where you stand.
You can never see out of my eyes.
I can only glimpse your experience
If you open your world to me,
And then it will only be a subtle flavour,
A fine texture, partly of my own creation

ONE WITH YOU

I don't want to draw you, photograph you,
Or even write a poem about you.
I want to be you, feel you deep in my being.
I want to touch you, become part of you.
I want to break down these barriers
And merge with you,
Experiencing your vastness, your completeness.

MISTAKEN

I have been mistaken
For I did not see you.
I did not take the time to explore you,
To plunge your depths
Or soar in your infinite skies.
And in this ignorance
Only suffering was born.
How many lifetimes will it take
To clear my debt to you?
My blindness did crush you,
But to return would be to destroy you completely.

WHAT SHALL I CALL YOU?

As I creep around you will be spiritual
As I work, you will be acupuncture
As I listen, you will be friendship
As I sleep you will be rest
As I eat you will be nourishment
As I die, you will have been my life.

FULL- BODIED

She wants to feel life,
To touch it, taste it
Full-bodied, multi-coloured, vibrant

NOT SO DIFFERENT

I see centipedes running heedlessly this way and that,
A hundred legs flailing about,
Turning in the same circles, getting nowhere.
I hear moths heading into the light,
Wings desperately flapping against the lampshade.
I see spiders curl up in fear, playing dead.
I see flies in the paint, unaware of the hand
That extends a possibility of escape –
Instead, they turn and walk further
Into their inevitable death.
At first – irritation –
Why do these creatures do these things
That cause them suffering?
Then, on closer inspection, I see myself.
In my own blind ignorance, I too run heedlessly,
Seduced by ever brighter lights,
Play dead and wade further into the mire,
All the while ignoring the extended hand
That offers to lead me to peace.

YELLOW SHOES

Yellow shoes outside the zendo door
Be mindful! Be a good student!
Enter zendo without a sound,
Bow in deep devotion
But where is the teacher?
Nowhere to be seen
Just yellow shoes outside this zendo door.

WHO WILL BE THERE?

Who will be there to hold me
In the depths of the darkest night?
Who will be there to guide me
When I'm blinded by too much light?
Who will be there to tell me its ok
When everything I've ever known
Slowly slips away?

THE RUG

I wish I could internalize you,
Make you an integral part of myself,
So that when you are gone
You don't take with you
The rug from under my feet.

OPEN

To remain open,
And indeed, to open more
In the face of my enemies, my fears,
This is my path

GETTING THROUGH THE DAY

Every moment, just this –
Eating, swallowing, hearing,
Seeing, walking, breathing,
Will this get me through each day?
But don't I want more than this?
More than walking with this paralyzing fear?
Is that enough?

THE ANSWER

I cannot find you in these books.
You were not there in her eyes,
Nor were you to be found in the zendo.
Without you I am nothing
With you I am no more
Where now must I turn?
But within.

A MOMENT OF BEAUTY

I feel the Buddha's hands,
Warm upon my back,
Inviting me to reach outwards
Into the centre of myself
And take his hand.
From either side I feel
The presence of my parents,
Warm ripples spread gently
Towards my heart.
As these beings touch,
So imperceptibly to be almost an illusion,
There is a breathtaking moment of beauty.
A moment where separation
And union fall away,
Revealing a place so fine and so subtle,
Yet so deep it holds the universe.

A SIMPLE LIFE

He smiles as he recounts his home life,
He looks forward to his evening with his lover.
He cooks, he cleans, he smokes,
What concerns has he?

She chants, she meditates,
She studies and strives,
Polishing her inner self.
But it can never shine quite brightly enough.

ATTACHMENT

It is all right to let go of you?
Distraction is your game.
It's good, even desirable
To banish you from my land.
But what of this "*spiritual practice*?"
Is there any stopping once begun?
Could we ever dare to tar you with the same brush?
Will it ever be all right to let you go?

PEACE

You say that peace is a fire.
This then must be my funeral pyre,
For I feel not a shred of life within this peace.

SHOW ME

Show me the passion in this silence
Show me the life in this stillness
Show me the joy in these tears
For I alone cannot find these qualities

THE BUDDHA'S PATH

I thought the Buddha's path
Lead from darkness to light,
But I have never known a darker sky

TSUNAMI

Know that not knowing brings pain
And knowing would bring a certain relief.
But all too quickly it gives way
To the all-consuming tidal wave of not knowing.
Ride it, relax into it, let it wash over you,
For it is bigger than you will ever be
And far more powerful.
Make it your friend
And you will never be alone.

RIGHT NOW

No place exists in space or time
Where everything will be all right.
There is no destination,
No road to travel.
Samsara, Nirvana, heaven and hell
Are one and nothing.
There is no end to suffering,
No moment of arriving.
This is really all there is.

FETTERED

I awake with a sleepy, dull mind,
And it is with a sleepy dull mind that I stand.
Restlessness pulls me to seek distractions,
And it is with this restlessness that I sit.
Dullness and laziness urge me to rest,
But it is with them that I walk.
Alertness and energy bubble within me,
And with these I lay.
Disinterested, I bend.
Fascinated, I stretch.
And so it goes,
And so I stay.

JUST BECAUSE

Just because I'm lost
Doesn’t mean that I don't know where I'm going.
Just because I’m treading water
Doesn’t mean I’m close to drowning.

HOW LONG?

How long will you go on pushing me?
And how long will I keep saying I'm sorry?
And how long will this voice within me
Keep telling me that it’s ok?
And when will I believe it?

WORTHY

All of my life to this moment has passed.
Whether I have lived it or not
Is open to debate.
How many more sunrises lie before me,
No one knows.
But what I do know is this -
That I will seize each day that comes,
Each moment,
And make it worthy of the title “life"

UNWORTHY

Cast adrift.
I have nothing to cling to.
Except the words of the Buddha,
But, unworthy,
I find no comfort there.

UNBEARABLE

I cannot bear to watch you dissolve again
I cannot bear to live with this constant contradiction
It is too much for me to take,
To feel you crumble in my hands,
No different to anything else.
Like sand you slip through my fingers
And this should be enough to set me free,
Yet still I yearn to believe

WISHING FOR A MR.BEN MOMENT

If only it were her life she was walking out of
And not merely just her front door.
If only she could step into a new world
Simply by taking off her hat

DOUBT

Why do I feel so dead? So unreal?
I thought the Buddha's path
Led from darkness to light,
But I have never known a darker sky.
You said I could transcend these feelings
That don't even belong to me,
But I don't know how.
You tell me to sit with it,
Breathe in and out,
Keep walking on.
But I have lived daily with it
For the whole of my life.
What good is it doing me to stay with it?
Please show me,
For I cannot see any benefit.
Is my life any easier or any better
For doing these daily practices?
I only feel greater confusion.

WAITING FOR YOU

I am waiting for you.
I have been waiting all my life,
But I do not know your name.
And shame on me,
For I would not recognize you if you came.

AN OBSERVATION

And how interesting
that life should leave its mark
as it slips ever more rapidly away

IF ONLY

If only you had stayed with me,
Given me a real pain with which to struggle.
Then maybe I could have kept at bay
This deeper pain within me.

INSIGNIFICANCE

I

The moon is magnificent,
Dressed in orange translucence.
I cannot bear to be so insignificant

II

Insignificance is its name,
Impotence its game

LOOK AGAIN

I see no significance to my life.
Look again, I implore you,
With eyes afresh.
Look again to truly see

THIS IS YOUR LIFE

Walking to work in the rain
This is your life
Sitting for hours
Watching the world fly by on the train
This is your life
Standing at the bus stop, waiting
This is your life
And no other
It does not start tomorrow
When everything is perfect
This is your life
Are you living it?

MIRROR

Be not a mirror to others
If you cannot bear to see
Your own self reflected back

WHAT ARE YOU CARRYING?

I have no choice
But to hold this tray,
For it has been given to me,
And if I look closely,
I can see that it was upon my demand.
But what I place upon it,
And indeed, how I carry it,
Are of my choosing

A GIFT

Let me give it to you
Like some precious gift
Allow you to take its weight
As I before you have done
Let me feel that release, that relief
As did those before me

PURE

There is a sadness
That weights upon my heart,
Nothing more.
Pure, undiluted
Almost raw.

ICE

You have no idea
How thin this ice beneath my feet
Or how deep these murky waters below
From which, if I were to slip,
I would never return

QUESTIONS

You say that I am fortunate
To be born a human being,
But in this moment I don't believe you.

You say that we have eyes to see
The wonder of this world,
I see only suffering.

You say we have ears to hear the divine,
I hear only screams from an inner hell.

You say we can open our heart
To feel incredible beauty,
I feel only intense pain.

You say I am fortunate
To be born a human being.

Yet I see birds hopping in the grass,
Careless it would seem,
Then take to wing and soar
In the vast blueness of the skies,
While I walk on wondering
At the purpose of my existence.
I see bees dive in and out of flowers,
Do they struggle daily with this crushing doubt?
I hear cuckoos sing their song,
Is theirs a song of confusion and angst?
I see spiders go about their business,
Do they spin webs that wrap them so tightly
That they cannot move?
You say these beings live in ignorance,
Living their lives driven by instinct, with no choice.
What choice do I have?
To stay, to go.
To live, to die
Suffering makes his home in all of these.

IS THERE ANYTHING LEFT HERE FOR ME?

Can she walk away
After all this time?
Can she just get up and walk away
Without a backward glance?
Can she walk away,
leave it all behind, and never return?
Will she ever know the answer to
"Is there anything left here for me?"

A PRAYER

May I wake each morning
with the song of joy in my heart,

May I greet the day's events
with respect and equanimity,

And may contentment be mine
with the setting of the sun.

~Thank you for reading ~

In March 2003, Michelle was offered a rare opportunity to live on a small Buddhist retreat centre in Wales. She packed up most of her belongings in a Fiat Cinquecento and made the journey that would change her life, but not in the way that she had expected.

Michelle wrote this collection of poems during her time at the retreat centre, whilst living in a very small caravan which overlooked the compost heap, at the bottom of the garden which she shared with a variety of spiders, crickets and moths, or it would be more precise to say that they shared it with her.

www.ingramcontent.com/pod-product-compliance
Ingram Content Group UK Ltd.
Pitfield, Milton Keynes, MK11 3LW, UK
UKHW020223250726
13967UKWH00001B/163